For we are God's masterpiece. He has created us anew in Christ Jesus, so we can do the good things he planned for us long ago.

Ephesians 2:10 (NLT)

For Bulk Order requests email: contact@adventuresofpookie.com

Printed in the United States of America
Paperback ISBN : 979-8-9850857-4-7
Hardcover ISBN: 979-8-9850857-5-4

www.AdventuresOfPookie.com

God's masterpiece

The Adventures of Pookie

Rebecca Yee

I am a work of art.
And you are a work of art.

When God created us in our mommy's tummy, he thought about every little detail.

He chose the colors of our skin,
hair, and eyes. He chose if we were
to be a boy or a girl.

Not one thing he created us to be is a mistake. He made us perfect.

Sometimes I feel like I don't fit in.
Sometimes I feel like people want
me to be someone else.

But...

I remember your word:
"I praise you because I am
fearfully and wonderfully made;
your works are wonderful I know
that full well." (Psalm 139:14 NIV)

We are wonderfully made.
God made us masterpieces.

He planned us long ago. He planned every little thing about us. And not only that, but he planned good things for us to do.

He loves us so much that he gave each of us a different talent to share with the world.

Some people like art, some people like music. Some people are good at sports, and some people are good at school.

Our gifts are unique to each one
of us. We are not like anyone else.

Just because you have a
different talent than your friends,
doesn't mean you aren't perfect.
It means you have a gift that
only you can have.

It doesn't matter what other people think of you, as long as you're doing what God wants you to do.

So don't be ashamed of your gift or try to use a different gift that's not yours.

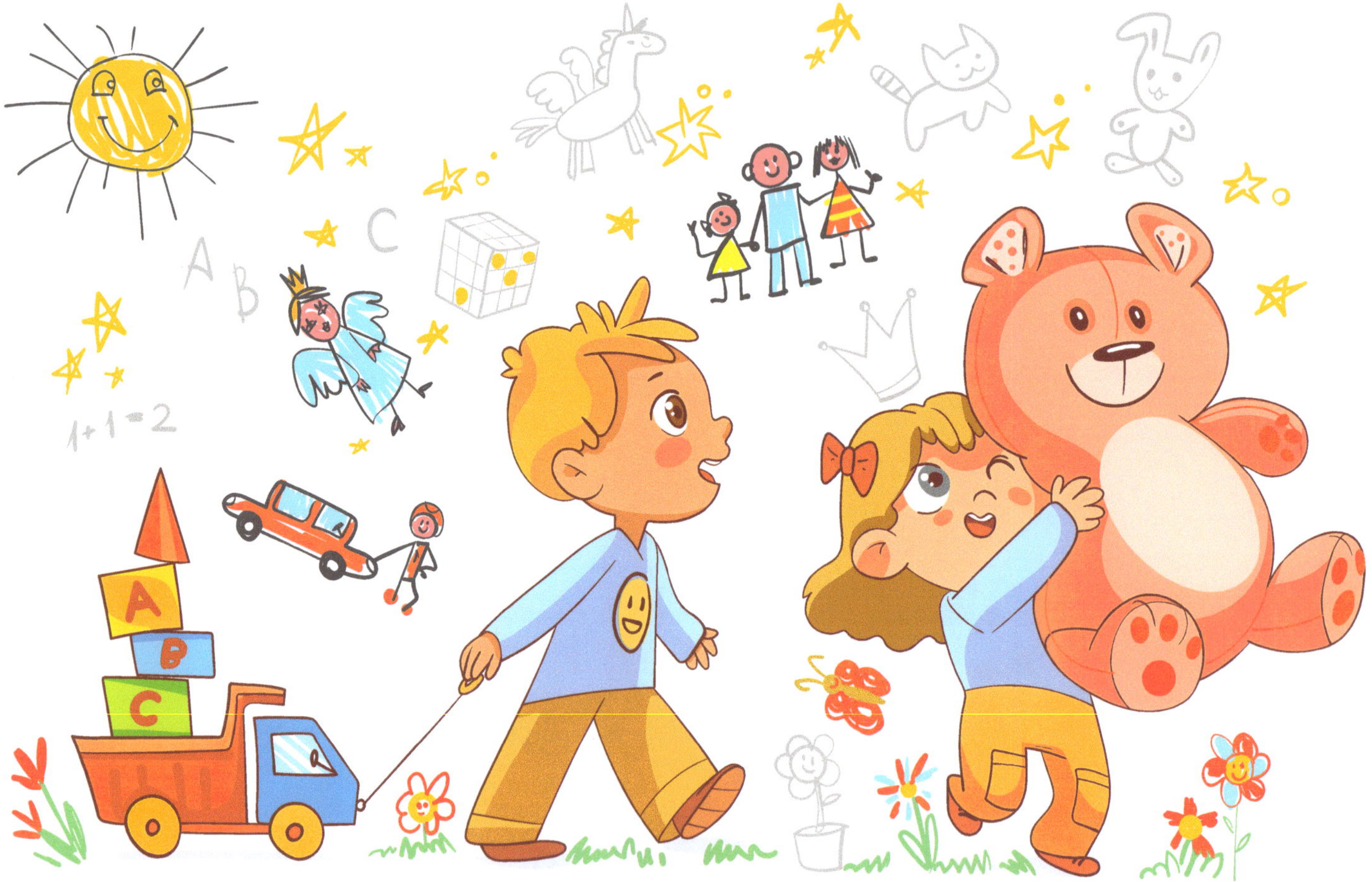
A B C
1+1=2
A
B
C

Stand tall and believe in
yourself always.

Because we are God's
Masterpieces and perfect in
every way.

I am
G☼d's
masterpiece

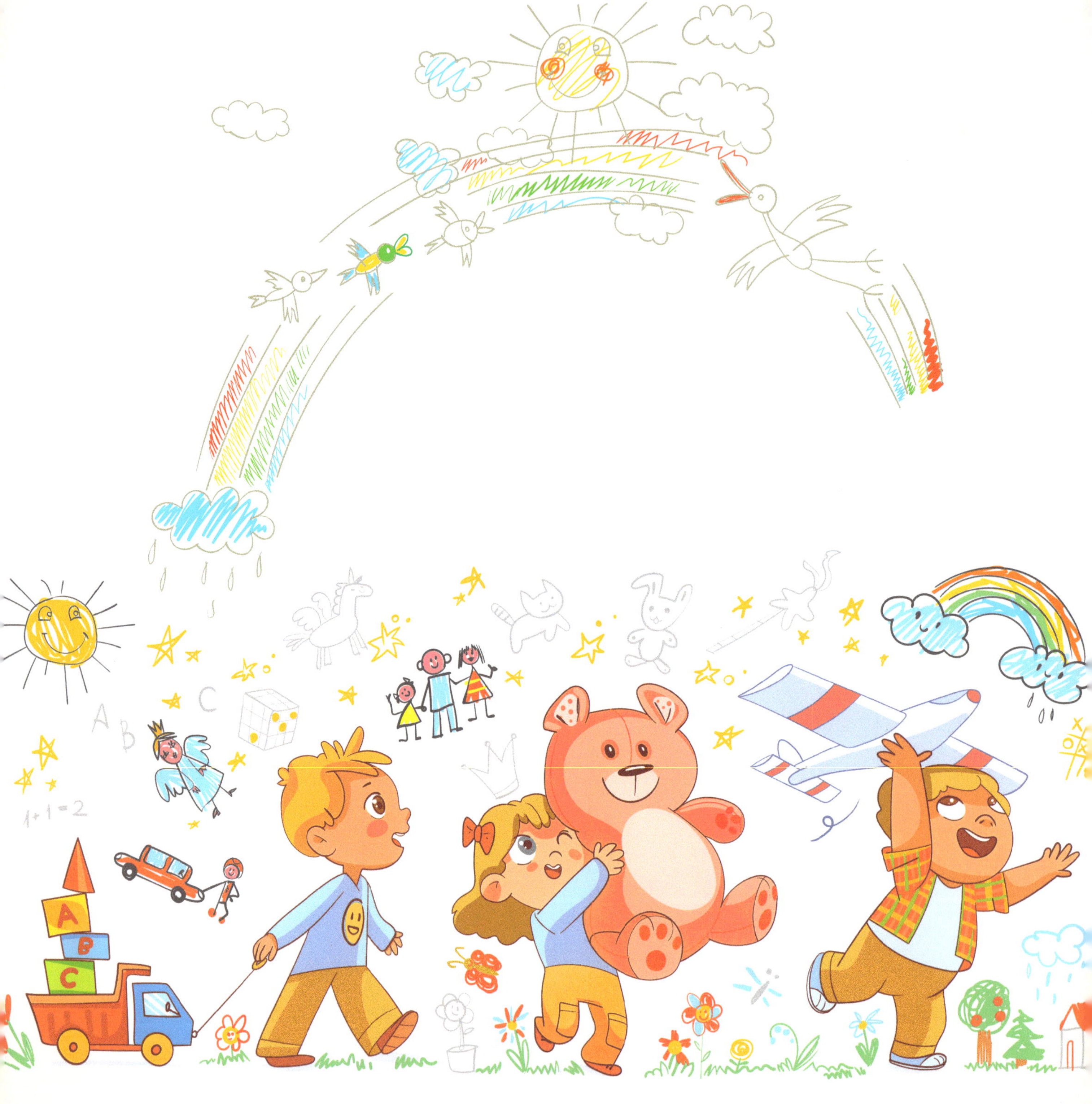
A B C
1+1=2
A
B
C

Download FREE Inspirational Printables at

AdventuresOfPookie.com

www.ingramcontent.com/pod-product-compliance
Lightning Source LLC
LaVergne TN
LVHW072056070426
835508LV00002B/122